Praise for *Life Is Funny but It Ain't No Joke*

Life Is Funny but It Ain't No Joke takes the reader on a healing journey to "be One with Self." RegE Walker does not "deliver" readers to a destination, but provides "spiritual prompts" or "guideposts" in the form of Wisdom Sayings to consider. While the sayings may seem deceptively simple, each provides an opportunity for us to reflect upon our values, choices, and actions. In a world where many of us yearn to heal and reconnect with our true selves, this book is a gift to help us discover who we truly are. It will help us return home.

Christina Robertson, Ph.D.
Career Consultant and Author, *A Woman's Guide to Divorce and Decision Making*

The much anticipated *Life Is Funny but It Ain't No Joke* gives the reader a snapshot of the author's path to enlightenment. In his down-to-earth manner, he artfully blends humor and sobering pearls of wisdom, much to the reader's delight. This book undertakes the classic struggle of the ego in its unending battle with the self, and you, the reader, have a front row seat. In his unique, awe-inspiring, easy-to-read style, RegE has provided us with serious thought-provoking material that is both inspiring and uniquely noteworthy.

Ponzi Watson Jr.
Chairman, Renaissance Management Group, Inc.
Advisory, Finance and Infrastructure Development

Life Is Funny but It Ain't No Joke is a beautiful and inspiring book by RegE Walker, a spiritual guide who admirably "walks his talk". He generously shares the wisdom gleaned from his own struggles and poignant journey of awakening. His stories and wisdom sayings are uplifting and encouraging, especially for anyone who seeks freedom from fear and doubt. This book is an invitation to embark on the "hero's journey" . . . but RegE lovingly warns that sometimes "going sane in an insane world feels like going crazy."

Christine Beardmore, D.Div.
Psychotherapist and Life Coach; President, The Inspired Life, LLC
Author, *The Inspiration Garden: Simple Ways to Grow a Good Life*

Mr. Walker's spiritual journey and the resultant wisdom sayings should uplift humanity. Copy your favorites and post them where you can pause and ponder their meaning throughout the day.

Lin Trower
Social Commentator

RegE makes a colorful case for the challenges and rewards of personal self-discovery. I found his life journey illuminating and his wisdom sayings awe-inspiring. While some made me laugh, others got a huge and humble Amen. Each saying took me to a different place inside and made me reflect. It was like a gentle smack on the head to help me remember who I am and why I am here. His work is a very practical guide for those on the road to discovery and rediscovery of who they are—young people, old people, and all those in between. Thank you RegE for such a delightful treat.

Helen Richardson, Ed.D.
Career Consciousness
Career and HR Coaching/Consulting/Training

Folks say, "The truth will set you free." But so often, the actual "wake up" calls jarringly disrupt our familiar identities/routines, trigger "heartburn," and make us feel miserable. RegE's transformative offering, *Life Is Funny but It Ain't No Joke*, however, invites compelling but gentle "wake ups"—the better for more thorough absorption, digestion and practical uplift. To heal our great planetary, collective, and personal divides, he challenges us . . . to own the depths of our conditioned minds . . . Like all addicts, we resist this healing journey, fearing that there may not be life after the death and pain of releasing all that we have previously believed about the world and who we have believed we were in it. His "identity theft" concept prepares us to shift out of "conditioned" striving to outrun life's perpetual "problems" into the "wake up" of delivering and pursuing the life solutions we know we love and need.

Thomas A. Gordon, Ph.D.
Psychologist and Leadership Coach, Thomas A. Gordon and Associates
Leadership solutions, change strategy, and performance navigation

For years, those of us who have been fortunate enough to know Mr. Walker have found in his foresight an irresistible mix of irony and insight, wisdom and wit, humor and heart. Whether they left us laughing or simply nodding our heads, his words encouraged us to go deeper and embrace our authentic selves. As a timely collection of his sayings and stories, *Life Is Funny but It Ain't No Joke* is a lighthouse, a North star, a set of guideposts to help us along life's most important mission: our spiritual journey.

Toussaint Losier, Ph.D.
Assistant Professor, Afro-American Studies, University of Massachusetts at Amherst

RegE Walker masterfully combines his ingenious writing style with his quick wit to bring us face to face with the realities of life. As you read *Life Is Funny but It Ain't No Joke* you catch a glimpse of the gold that has always flowed through the core of his being. His own life experience, coupled with his courage to awaken, led him to this treasure trove of gems that appears before you. The "Wisdom Sayings" are pure Gold. For RegE, his awakening continues; for us, just like in the "hero's journey" he continues to bestow his blessings on all he meets along the way.

Rev. Sheila E. Pierce
Founding Senior Minister, The Center of Peace, Centers for Spiritual Living

LIFE IS FUNNY

but

It Ain't No Joke

A Journey of Awakening Through Wisdom Sayings

Reg E Walker

Harmanity Press • www.harmanitypress.com
Available for purchase from Amazon.com and other retail outlets
First Edition
© 2016, 2020 by Reginald E. Walker

ISBN: 978-1537458311

Copyediting: Darryl Farrar, Daniel J. King, and James Solomon
Production Manager, Book Design, and Typesetting: Mark Parker Miller
Cover Design: Rohaan Malhotra
Lotus Photograph: John Creveling
Some designs adapted from Geoffrey Williams, *African Designs from Traditional Sources* (Dover Publications, 1971)

Subjects: SPIRITUALITY; WISDOM SAYINGS; SELF IDENTITY; SELF HELP

***The ladies in my life**
Grandmother, Cornelia, my rock of ages
Mother, Thelma, my guardian angel
Wife, Gerri, my joy
Daughter, Rana "Bush," my spirit twin*
and the men
*Grandfather, Jesse "Pat," a gentle soul
Father, Charles, a path finder
Son, Tschaka "Duff," a truth seeker*

Contents

Introduction

The inspiration for this book grew out of a talk I had with one of my students in the garden of my home. Among the things we talked about was the way the mind (through the ego) is able to assume one's identity and—like the machine in the film *The Matrix*—siphon off its unsuspecting victim's energy to serve its own insidious agenda.

Sometime after our talk, I felt compelled to write what later became the first section of **Life Is Funny but It Ain't No Joke.** The "Identity Theft" parable is the story of what happens to a person who forgets their true identity and then mistakenly identifies with the mind as their self and the dire consequences that follow, including sleepwalking through one's entire life.

The initial section is followed by my spiritual autobiographical sketch, "Journey to Freedom." In it I briefly describe my spiritual odyssey, which the great mythologist Joseph Campbell called the hero's journey. In his book of the same name, Campbell explains how those who successfully complete this phase of the great awakening return from their venture within endowed with the power to bestow blessings on others.

The seed of the "Wisdom Sayings" portion of *Life Is Funny but It Ain't No Joke* was actually planted years before I conceived of the previous two sections and long before I had any inkling that one day I would write this book. The awareness that what I said in conversation often contained words of wisdom that should be recorded was first brought to my attention by Ranjit Bhattacharya, a young man from India who rode with me every day to Lincoln University in Pennsylvania, where he was a lab assistant and

I was a guidance counselor. Once I acknowledged the value of the insights, my companion and I developed a system: I drove and talked, and he recorded the **wisdom sayings**, as I call them. When we reached campus, my spiritual assistant would present me with a page with the day's catch of pearls of wisdom.

The wisdom sayings are designed to allow you to bypass your conditioned mind and reconnect directly with your *true identity*. This powerful, spiritual reunion with *Self* will inspire as well as challenge you to reclaim the authentic life you were born to live.

"Know Thy Self," the concluding section of the book, is a compilation of the testimonies of preeminent spiritual voices throughout the ages that bear witness to the truth of who we are.

Reg E Walker

This book is the door of return to your *true identity*.

Heal Thy self*

To make whole is to heal
To heal is to reconnect
To reconnect is to remember who you are
To remember who you are is to know why you are here
To know why you are here is to know what you do
To know what you do is to realize your divine mission
To realize your divine mission is to be One with SELF**

* Refers to the everyday self, your personality (see lowercase *self*, p. 183).

** Refers to the spiritual SELF, your Divine nature, the real YOU, the impersonal, universal YOU (see uppercase *Self*, p. 183, for other iterations).

Identity Theft

The Parable of the Homeless *soul*

From birth, Soula was endowed with a Divine estate (*kingdom within*). His was a place where he was whole, lacking no-thing to be complete, and happy. Due to the grandeur of his estate, it was run by a staff led by headly, the head man, and his loyal assistant, hego. In time, Soula grew restless and longed to explore the wonders of the world beyond his estate. The more Soula was attracted to this new world, the less often did he experience the old familiar feeling of being whole and at peace. He soon began to feel that something was missing, something he could not identify but was convinced could only be found in the world outside his domain.

Before setting off on his search, Soula went over the care and upkeep of his Divine estate during his absence with his loyal servant headly (conditioned mind), who had been second in charge from the very beginning. With headly's assurance that he and his loyal assistant, hego (ego), would take care of everything *as if it were their own*, Soula was on his way.

At first, Soula maintained a steady correspondence with his household, showing a keen interest in how things were being run. But the more entranced he became by the wonders of his new life, the more *he forgot about home, eventually cutting off all contact with his Divine estate.* **soula*** now spent all of his waking hours seeking that something he *believed* he was lacking to be whole and happy again.

* soula (with lowercase "s") refers to the soul when it is no longer connected to its True Identity.

2

He vowed to himself that he would not return home until he had discovered, in the world outside, that missing something that would permanently end his search. Whenever soula had doubts about having left home, he persuaded himself that all was indeed well. Weren't **Headly***and hego looking after his estate as if it were their own? Why worry? So soula dismissed his concerns and doggedly carried on.

After years of being entranced by one thing and then another in the outside world, but not discovering anything that permanently ended his search for that one thing he prayed would restore him to his original state of well-being, soula was forced to admit to himself that he had failed. Certainly, he had enjoyed a countless number of new and exciting experiences and momentary pleasures, but none brought him the

---

* Headly (with uppercase "H") refers to the mind when it has usurped the True Identity of the soul.

lasting feeling of being whole and happy he so longed for. Without fail, his initial joy—in discovering what he believed was that missing something—turned to disappointment when that awful craving for something more returned to haunt his every step. Relentlessly, it drove him on in search of that next thing that would finally bring his desperate search to an end.

Exhausted and impoverished by his endless journey and slightly bent by the mounting weight of his never-ending search, soula finally came to the realization that *in a world of impermanence, nothing of permanence can ever be found!* Finally awakened from his slumber by this startling revelation, soula joyfully turned toward home, where he now remembered wanting nothing and being whole and happy.

When at long last he arrived at his Divine estate, he was instructed by a small brass plate on the great door to ring bell for entry. He rang and waited. But soula was not prepared for what happened next: when the door opened, soula could plainly see that hego, Headly's loyal assistant, was dressed in the clothes of the lord of the estate—his clothes! To add to his shock and dismay, not only did hego not welcome him warmly, he greeted soula as a stranger and commoner with a chilling, "And what can I do for you?" To this, a stunned soula replied, "Don't you recognize me, hego? It is I, soula, the lord of the estate, returning after many years of seeking in the outside world that which I already had at home." To this, a sneering hego responded, as he straightened *his* tie and looked coldly into his former master's eyes, "I don't think so! My master, Headly, is the lord of this estate." He then slammed the great door shut in his former master's bewildered face.

Feeling betrayed, soula began to pound on the great door and scream after hego, demanding that he be allowed entry into his Divine estate. When no response was forthcoming, soula did not know where next to turn, *as he had depended on Headly and his loyal assistant for everything.* He now assumed his fate was sealed and all was lost. Unaware that Headly could never permanently claim his divine birthright, a defeated soula returned once more to the world of *impermanence* from which he had so recently sought refuge. There he again joined the ranks of those *homeless* souls whose true identity had also been usurped by one that was intended to serve.

Journey to Freedom

The Hero's Journey

What you believe can move a mountain
*or **put one in your way***

My spiritual journey began with a deep longing . . . a hunger to know if there was more to me, to us, than meets the eye. There had to be more than just a brain, five senses, and a body to explain the strange things I had experienced and heard about.

There was Edgar Cayce, the famous psychic who was known as the "Sleeping Prophet." While in an altered state, Cayce would render health and life "readings" for those who sought him out after the mainstream medical and religious establishments had failed to adequately address their concerns. His accomplishments were more amazing when you consider that his "patients" often were not even in his presence!

And what about the not-so-famous healers like my uncle Willie, a fire-and-brimstone preacher from the old South who, I was told, healed me of a potentially fatal infant illness through the power of prayer? Perhaps it was this miraculous healing way back then that awakened in my soul the conviction that we are far more than just flesh and blood.

Asleep at the Wheel

I remember hearing in church during my youth that we were all God's children and recall thinking, if we have the same

DNA as our Creator, *then we all must be Gods in the making!* And isn't it written somewhere in the Bible that Jesus, the Son, promised His disciples they would perform even greater wonders than He had? Since I considered myself something of a disciple, having been raised in the church and a true believer, it was easy to persuade myself that His promise applied to more than just the original twelve.

Inspired by my belief, I set off during my twenties in search of the *Source* of the transformative power I hoped would liberate me from a limited sense of myself and life's possibilities. After an ill-conceived and halfhearted search, I concluded that knowledge of the Source was lost to us moderns, buried long ago with the ancients.

Then sometime after my failed first attempt, I started hearing the words to an old church song repeating in my head:

"Ezekiel saw a wheel way up in the middle of the air . . ." Those words kept running through my mind until I was compelled to look up Ezekiel in the Bible and see just what he said. What I found in Ezekiel 1:16 and 17 is what I believe to have been his encounter with a UFO: "This was the appearance of the wheel: They sparkled like chrysolite, and all four looked alike. Each appeared to be made like a wheel intersecting a wheel. As they moved, they would go in any one of the four directions the creatures faced." This and other writings became the foundation for my belief that alien visitations to our planet had been occurring at least since biblical times. It then required but a small leap, from the acceptance of the existence of aliens, to the conclusion they held the key to our future. It wasn't long before I began to think of them as elder brothers—no, avatars or saviors here to establish contact with us through abductees, who they used to convey the knowledge we need to quicken our evolution and revolutionize how we must live on Earth.

But the real reward of my study of the UFO phenomenon was the opportunity to speculate on the existence of worlds beyond our own and to imagine how their inhabitants live and what they might think.

This dramatic shift in my thinking allowed me to challenge much of what I had been taught as absolute truth during the innocence of youth. I even began to wonder if these extraterrestrial beings worshipped the same tribal gods we did or if they worshipped gods at all! Ultimately, I decided that if there are other worlds, it is unlikely their inhabitants believe and live as we do.

And if there are no worlds beyond our own, my exploration of "outer space" had at least afforded me the opportunity to begin to think outside the *closed belief system* that, until then, had determined my identity and fate. As a result of intense probing over time, I overturned much of what I had been taught and unknowingly undermined my conditioned state of mind.

Dying to Live

It happened on a fateful fall evening in 1968. I experienced a shift in consciousness so profound that I have no name for but *It*. I was sitting on our old green couch in the small space that served as both dining and living room in the apartment my wife and I first called home. At some point, I nodded off and slipped into a corner of myself where I had never been. Somehow, I made a breakthrough or had a breakdown—at the time, I knew not which. I stumbled beyond the boundary of accepted sanity into a no man's land inside myself and crossed the border of my conditioned mind into a zone forbidden to all except mental and religious authorities—anointed by society to reclaim lost souls for *its* purposes and not for the benefit of those who were troubled or deemed lost . . .

There I sat, frozen inside myself, terrified by an unbearable sound, like the roar of a jet engine, that was accompanied by a bright light continuously changing from yellow to green to red and colors I no longer recall. Each time the light changed, a scene from my past clicked into view like a slide in a projector. These familiar images exposed me to a chilling reality I was ill-prepared to face: my life was not of my own conscious making. I was forced to come face to face with the reality that *I made nothing happen; everything had happened to me!* My life had been unfolding according to the dictates of this thing—this cold, impersonal, unbelievably loud machine, with its alternating colored light. While I was asleep (unconscious), this life form had captured my consciousness and was living through me. Because my eyes were open, I was lulled into believing that I was awake. But like a total eclipse of the sun, this dark, unknown presence had blotted out the light of my true nature.

Mercifully, I was finally released from the terror inside me. It seemed to last a lifetime but, for all I know, was merely a split second. I tried to convince myself *It* didn't happen, but from inside I heard a still, small voice that I couldn't ignore: *This truth cannot be denied!* In a flash, all my cherished beliefs and values, and with them my identity, vanished. The compass that had guided me through life was no more. I no longer had any idea who I was, where I was headed, or even the sensation of being alive. I was a shell of my former self, a proverbial dead man walking. Yet, at the time of the death of who I *believed* I was, I could only mourn. After all, that self was the only me I knew.

Delusions die hard and, in dying, can make you feel like you're dying with them. That's how I felt with the death of my false self. My feelings of loss and devastation were so intense I could hardly bear them. It was as if an enormous weight had fallen on my shoulders and, at any moment, I would be crushed under this overwhelming burden I was forced to bear. The pressure was so great that for several days I *literally* could not stand erect. My belief in a God outside—up in heaven, protecting me—was gone! The faith of my forefathers, which had been my rock, crumbled into dust and was replaced by fear, self-loathing, and a feeling that I had been cast aside, abandoned by my God. I was on my own. Alone! without faith in the cosmos or confidence in myself. Still, out of habit and fear of impending doom,

I cried out, "God, where am I? Save me. I'm lost!" How I felt is best expressed by a saying familiar to many who have experienced the dark night of the soul: *Religion is for those who fear going to hell; spirituality is for those who've been there!*

The morning after the death of my innocence, I headed straight to my parents' house. While sitting at the foot of their bed, I explained to Mom, as best I could, the previous night's soul-wrenching experience of how I got lost. I turned to Mom because I knew she would somehow be able to help me understand what had happened. After hearing me out, she sat straight up in bed. Then staring just above my head, with a look of fierce determination and defiance in her voice, she said, "I see an old man standing over you. He's pressing down on your shoulders. You must fight him. He's trying to take over. Don't let him!"

I was grateful for my mother's gift of clairvoyance (second sight) and the dramatic way she made me aware of the seriousness of the challenge I faced. It was now up to me to find a way to escape from this energy-thirsty vampire . . .

As "luck" would have it, I came across renowned psychiatrist Carl Jung's autobiography, *Memories, Dreams, Reflections*. In his book, he describes "personality No. 2" as an unconscious entity that lives in the past and shadows personality No. 1, which lives in the here and now and connects us to everyday life. From Jung's description, I concluded his No. 2 was the same old man Mom had "seen" standing over me. It was this powerful energy form, which had erupted from the depths of my psyche, intent on disconnecting me from No. 1. Somehow I knew if No. 2 were to have its way, I would be cut off from the worldly aspect of myself and, like so many before, lost to the life I knew forever.

Becoming sane in an insane world feels like going crazy. Slowly, yet oh so painfully, I began to draw back from the edge of personal extinction and make sense of that terrifying experience, which in the blink of an eye had changed the course of my life. In time, I came to understand that, by undermining my conditioned state of mind, I had not only uprooted many of my earlier, self-limiting beliefs but had unwittingly unleashed a hell-bent intruder that now engaged me in a struggle for my very sanity and life as I knew it.

As for that droning, unbearably loud "machine," I discovered it was my mind. My encounter with it forced me to realize that the mind is a machine, but a machine without an operator.

It is a builder, but a builder without a plan. Impersonal and amoral by its very nature, it is incapable of judging the worth of materials. It is the responsibility of the architect of one's life to provide the mind with a blueprint, as it will build with any thought, belief, feeling, or experience—be it self-empowering or self-sabotaging. I also began to think of the mind as a kind of personal computer and realized that if the owner-operator is not programming it, the rest of the world is!

I later concluded the flashing light that changed colors—each time revealing a different scene from my past—was the ego-driven aspect of my mind. **The ego, or false self, gradually gains control as its host forgets who they truly are (falls asleep) and tragically identifies with the mind as their self.** I believe it is this grave error in consciousness that enables the mind, through its surrogate, the ego or *mind-made self*, to assume its host's identity and redirect the unsuspecting victim's energy to serve the mind's own reality-distorting agenda.

Forgetting who I AM came easily because, like almost everyone else, I was persuaded by those around me—who were already asleep—to reject and eventually forget the true me. At every turn, I was force-fed the notion that I was nothing in and of myself, that everything of real and lasting value existed outside of me. I was just another machine, a more sophisticated machine than had yet been created: a brain, five senses, and a body, but a machine and nothing more. As a result of my cultural conditioning, I unconsciously embraced the **belief** that in order to be somebody, I had to make something of myself as defined by society's standards. Gradually, I was seduced by the all-consuming ideal that the key to happiness lay in the development of my intellect, the health and fitness of my physical body, and accomplishment in the outer world. The more I surrendered to these external ideals, the more my awareness and energy were focused on the world and not on me. Trapped in this never-ending struggle to validate myself according to society's dictates, I simply forgot who I AM and, in time, lost my way, much as Soula had in the Identity Theft parable.

What ultimately saved me from complete spiritual annihilation was the awareness that I could not be my mind, as it was *I* who helplessly watched as my mind pursued a course of action without my conscious consent. Because I was conditioned to believe that my mind was me, how could I even begin to ask whether what was in it's interest was not best for me? *Rather than living my authentic life, I had been living the life of my mind!* Like just about everyone else in our culture, I was addicted to my mind for just about everything, even "reasons of the heart that reason cannot understand."

In my ongoing struggle to make sense of what happened to me on that terrifying night, I eventually realized *I* am not my body either. When I reflect back on that delusion-shattering experience, I recall that my body was asleep while *I* was forced to witness my mind in action. As a result of this realization, I began to think of my body as a kind of outer garment.

Like the other planets in our solar system, ours is out there in space, orbiting the sun. In order for us to function on Earth, Mother Nature has clothed us in a body, or what I like to call a perma-wear space suit. This incredible, one-of-a-kind body-suit grows with us and, if damaged, can normally repair itself. It is this remarkable creation that allows us to fully participate in life on our planet.

Thanks to my rude awakening, I was now aware that *I* existed separate and apart from my mind, its ego, and my body. Because I no longer identified with who I formerly *believed* I was, my spiritual amnesia was beginning to end. But I still did not know who I was. And to make this discovery, I would have to undertake a journey that was no longer in the outer world. Unlike what I was conditioned to believe in the past, the path to my spiritual liberation—the discovery of my true identity, personal power, and authentic life—would begin *within*.

The Road Less Traveled

The first great obstacle I encountered, even before my venture inward began, was FEAR—fear brought on by my belief that I would find nothing of real and permanent value inside me. At best, I expected to find something less worthy than my mind, its ego, and my body with which to identify. Although fearful of what I might find, I was committed to undertaking the quest. What did it matter, anyway? The life I was leaving behind was a spiritual wasteland! So began the journey in the direction I hoped would lead to my spiritual reclamation.

As I turned my awareness inward, I was encouraged and gently guided every step—at least when I was trusting enough to allow myself to be led. The first time I surrendered to guidance, I was on a Trailways bus headed to Harlem, New York, to meet with a group of African nationalists. This was shortly after having been stripped of my old, false identity and all I believed in and cherished and left naked and so utterly broken that the only thing I could think about was ending it all. That was when I again heard the voice of salvation from deep within my core now declare: *You are not that selfish.* My encounter with this *Presence* forced me to recognize that although I could no longer see the value of my own life, others did. In time, it would become clear to me just how selfish it would have been to escape by ending my life rather than meeting the challenge of living on in the face of my identity-shattering loss. It was those closest to me who would suffer, be heartbroken, and have to live in shame if I had snuffed out my own *Light*.

Not long after resigning to live, my conscious mind began to be renewed by a stream of healing wisdom sayings from some previously untapped *spiritual* wellspring. The first, "A Love Supreme: patience, generosity, and courage are not required of one who truly loves." This enabled me to appreciate the adage that love truly does conquer all; that if I learn to love myself and live out my passion, everything would unfold as it should. Another early one, "You must take responsibility for the actions of your mind," reaffirmed that I am not my mind but its master. I am responsible for it, not it for me. As I grew more grounded and self-assured, I was struck by an even more sobering wisdom saying: "You are ultimately responsible for who you are and the quality of your life. You are the final authority." Or, as my father, a Baptist minister, later put it, "Each of us is our own messiah!" The more receptive I was to these words of wisdom, the less fearful and the more inspired and empowered I became. **By embracing wisdom sayings in my thinking, I was able to free my mind of the grip of self-limiting beliefs and to discover that I now had the final say!** Wisdom sayings then started flowing into my newly expanded mind at such an unrelenting pace, I had to scramble to write them down anytime, anyplace, on any scrap of paper I could find. In time I would come to understand their value to others, but at that moment I knew only they were saving me.

A Dream Deferred

In August of 1969, at the urging of Noah Robinson, an acquaintance who was in Wharton's MBA program, I enrolled in the University of Pennsylvania's new, innovative program, which served as a bridge into university life. After one semester in Community Wharton Education Program, I was offered a scholarship that would allow me to complete the last two years of my degree. However, to receive it, I first had to get a C or better in Russian 102. I was required to take 102 because, three years earlier, at LaSalle College (now University), I had received an incomplete in Russian 101, and it wasn't being offered in the evening that semester at Penn. Instead of registering for classes back in the spring of 1966 at LaSalle and removing the "I" from my transcript, I chose instead to answer the call to join the ranks of the history makers of my generation and headed to Atlanta, Georgia, and became a member of the Student Nonviolent Coordinating Committee (SNCC).

When I returned home, in late July or early August of that year, I had no intention of ever sitting my butt in another American classroom. I was disheartened by the blatant racial hatred I witnessed and experienced in Greene County, Alabama, where I was assigned, and during the March Against Fear in Mississippi. The march was led by Dr. King and other civil rights leaders after a cowardly, redneck sniper wounded James Meredith as he attempted to walk solo across the state.* It was during this march that Stokely Carmichael (Kwame Ture) of SNCC, a classmate from my Howard University days, popularized the

* James Meredith was the first student of African descent to integrate the all-white University of Mississippi in 1962.

phrase "Black Power!" Given my feelings of shame and disappointment toward the country of my birth, I wasn't about to answer his call to action by working toward some vague future when black folk might have real power in America. I wanted mine NOW! And to get it, I was prepared to pack the few things I owned and stake my claim to a share of black power in Ghana, West Africa. I'd had my fill of the stark inequalities and the racism that fueled white indifference and outright hostility to our progress.

Despite my intention to permanently move to Africa, that dream was deferred until 1976, as I was about to enter the University of Pennsylvania—that is, remember, if I got a C in Russian 102. But get this! In order to be prepared for 102, I had to relearn Russian 101's seventeen chapters over a three-week Christmas break and be ready to hit the ground running. To complicate matters,

I was married and the father of two small children and running an African import and gift shop. On top of that, the dean of academic affairs, after reviewing my transcript, called me in for a reality check! With only a passing nod to my two years of college, she turned her attention to my SAT scores. They were an anemic 685. That's right, a combined 685 out of a possible 1600! And in her eyes, I had committed a crime of equal magnitude: I was the product of Simon Gratz, an all-black, inner-city high school. But the final clue to my inevitable demise was my grade on Penn's math aptitude test. My score revealed that my math proficiency was equivalent to that of a high school freshman. This, along with everything else, convinced the good dean that I was not going to cut it competing alongside young, white, privileged Ivy Leaguers.

Since I was already an entrepreneur with ambitions of one day living and doing business in Africa, my heart was set on completing my degree at Penn's prestigious Wharton School of Business. Given my shaky scores and credentials, I could definitely see why the dean felt it her duty to persuade me to stay the hell away from that esteemed institution. In her mind, I was clearly a disaster looking for a place to crash and burn, and she didn't want the remains of my black ass scattered all over the hallowed halls of Wharton. Thankfully, the decision was not hers to make. As the final authority in my own life, I chose to follow my dream. Wharton it was! With a tone of impending doom in her voice (leaving unspoken the words she undoubtedly was thinking, *you'll never make it!*), she sent me on my way with a dismissive "Well, hitch your wagon to a star . . ."

And did I ever! While continuing to operate my business, I completed the required seventeen chapters of Russian in three weeks and jumped right into the evening class. That first night, as

I entered the classroom and was about to take a seat, the instructor immediately got up from his and, in a voice quavering with contempt, cut right into me: "Mr. Walker, as you are well aware, you have missed the whole first semester. I, therefore, sincerely doubt that you will be able to keep up with the class. With that in mind, I'm putting you on notice: You are not welcome in this class! If you choose to disregard my advice and remain, do not expect me to adjust [i.e., slow] the pace of the course work to accommodate you." I just sat there, consumed by embarrassment and then rage. But I was on a mission, and the words of an old movement song, "ain't gonna let nobody turn me round, turn me round . . . ," soothed my wounded ego and brought me back to the reality of the challenge that lay ahead—beginning that very night!

It was this same professor, on the last night of class, who proposed a toast to me as the two of us sat in the White Dog

Café, finishing off several rounds of vodka. He informed me that he had checked the Slavic Department's records and found that no student entering a Russian class at mid-year had performed as well as I had. (My grade for the course was a solid B.) Wharton day school, here I come! During the balance of my time at Penn, I performed enough outstanding academic feats to be convinced that I had somehow tapped into some as yet unidentified, amazing, *higher power*.

An unexpected, yet welcome, blessing of my time at Penn was finally defeating the "old man," as my mother called it. I suspect its demise was the result of me being forced by my business studies to depend primarily on the rational side of my brain rather than the intuitive, which I had deferred to almost exclusively in recent years. Perhaps it was this new pattern of mental engagement that rebalanced my psychic forces and vanquished that shadowy presence back to the underworld from where it had so forcefully and frighteningly emerged.

New Birth in Africa

Seven months after graduating from Penn and some four years after the trauma of my awakening from the great sleep, I checked into a small room in a third-class hotel in Addis Ababa, the capital of Ethiopia. Ethiopia was the sixteenth country on my eight-month grand tour of Western Europe and the continent of Africa. I landed in Addis after a month or so in Wao, a town in southern Sudan.* Wao is home to the Dinka, a Nilotic people reputed to be the descendants of the mighty, ancient empire of Kush. It was there among the Dinka that I witnessed the last gen-

---

* In 2011, southern Sudan became the Republic of South Sudan.

erations of those who are sustained by a traditional way of life that is rapidly disappearing from the African scene. Years later I realized that in some ways their journey mirrored my own: a passing away of the old without having yet given birth to the new . . .

Back in the States, I had persuaded myself that the reason for my trip abroad was to experience firsthand the European and African currents of my bloodlines and to explore the entrepreneurial opportunities I assumed awaited someone with my Wharton education, five years of business experience, and passion for Africa. A deeper, spiritual reason did not reveal itself until I was well on my way—I needed time away from everybody and everything familiar in order to figure out and get acquainted with who I was becoming. I was dead to my former, false self but had no indication how, when, or where my second coming might occur and who I would be.

On my first or second day in Addis, July 4th or 5th of 1972, I stopped to browse in a little bookstore down the hill from my hotel. I remember picking up two books and being unable to decide which to buy. One was on African development; I don't recall its title or author. The other was *What Life Should Mean to You* by Alfred Adler. Adler, like Jung, was a famous psychiatrist and former disciple of Sigmund Freud. I bought neither then but returned to my hotel. I was clearly at a cross-roads in my life and had to choose between my twin passions of spirituality (the transformation of human consciousness) and my appetite for all things African. Surrendering to guidance, I chose spirituality. That was indeed a fortuitous choice as, that very evening, Adler's book turned out to be the catalyst for my second spiritual breakthrough in four years.

I devoured his book in a single sitting and was then prompted by a familiar inner *Presence* to prepare to record whatever was about to come through. With notebook and pen in hand, I sat on the side of my bed ready to receive further insight into a transformation that was changing me from the inside out. And then it began . . .

The Addis Transmission

Self Revelation and Life's Work

You are not who society or your friends or your family see you as. You are not who you imagined yourself to be. You are the transformative power of insight. You must stay true to yourself and your calling to help others remember they are SPIRITUAL BEINGS CLOTHED IN HUMAN FORM. Know that you have all that you need to succeed. Whenever you question the value of your life's work, remember that those who feed others never go hungry. Know that, regardless of your past, you are always on your path.

I was also challenged to examine several areas of my life where I needed to grow in order to realize a greater measure of my potential:

Life Challenges

Be open to others. Their talents, experience, and goodwill help you make your way in the world. Stop worrying, as you know from past experience that nothing is as hard or as bad as it seems. Accept that, as the final authority in your own life, you are the Source of your happiness as well as your pain and suffering. Remember the Power is not only within. You are that Power! Never forget: You only receive what you truly believe you are worthy of. All is well.

And just like that, the transmission ended.

As I sat there that night, looking out at the lights of Addis, I suddenly realized *I had entered a realm of inner calm and joy, of lightness and a profound sense of security and love, the likes of which I had never before nor since experienced.* Maybe I was feeling loved and secure the whole time I was transcribing but took no notice until the session's end. *In that timeless moment, I was at peace with all of creation and One with Self. There were no boundaries. All was formless. There was no more longing, no fear. I was whole. I was happy. I was free!* Surely, if there is a heaven, I've already been there.

On that African night, now holy to me, in a small room in an Ethiopian hotel, I was reunited with *Self,* the Source of that sought-after power of personal transformation. Though full of doubt and fear at the beginning of my journey, I had, nevertheless, gone in search of the Source and discovered the *Source and*

I are One! After four years and a lifetime, my faith in my Divine nature and the universe had been restored!

Yet two questions remained: Why had it taken so long, and why did I suffer so much before I was able to acknowledge and embrace my divinity—my power and authority? Perhaps because I was conditioned to fear it, deny it, or attribute it exclusively to a select few by those who are unaware of, or afraid to embrace, their own. Maybe it's just as my wife has so often reminded me by quoting one of my own wisdom sayings, "Nothing happens before its time, and when it's time, nothing else can happen!"

As a way of confirming the reality of my reunion with *Self,* while undressing for bed that night, I was led in that moment by who I really am—*not dictated to by some alien voice in my head*—to remove all the valuables from my pockets, place them on the bureau, and leave my room door not just unlocked but wide open, in a third-class hotel in the heart of Addis! When I awoke the next morning, all my valuables were where I had left them, and I was still enveloped in the afterglow of my *spiritual rebirth* from the night before. I took this demonstration as *Self*'s way of assuring me that when I surrender to divine guidance I am always protected. But over the following days, the activities, the doubts, the questions, and the shadow of my old companion, Fear, returned to challenge the reality of my extraordinary, "out of mind" experience. I found myself drifting back toward the prison of my old, familiar, limited state of mind, but not all the way back. I had experienced the height of my Being, and I would never go completely back to sleep and live in total ignorance (darkness) of who I AM in truth—*Self*, that Divine Essence that is known by many names . . .

Having completed what the great mythologist Joseph Campbell called "the hero's journey," I returned to those I had left behind, bearing gifts of *Spirit* that even now continue to flow forth from reuniting with *Self*. In addition to the outpouring of self-liberating, healing wisdom sayings that began with the death of my false identity some four years earlier, my spiritual awakening revealed that I am a teacher, a healer, and a spiritual guide. An unusual gift of my new life is being chosen, on occasion, by friends on the other side to act as a channel during dreams, to convey to grieving loved ones on this side that by "dying" they have merely crossed over to the spiritual realm where there is *life* after life. Moreover, since answering the call of destiny, the central motif of my life's work has been helping others to remember who they are in truth.

In four years and a lifetime, I had traveled from the depths of utter despair to a glimpse of my *true identity*. What I once thought was the worst thing that could happen—the death of who I **believed** I was—has turned out to be my greatest good. Now I am free to say yes to my highest good, to *Self*, and its awesome power to liberate me from a limited sense of myself and life's possibilities.

You know the way. Now undertake the journey to reclaim your Divine estate. As a seeker of your spiritual birthright, you must embark on a journey of SELF* recovery beyond attachment to who you have been conditioned to *believe* you are: your mind, ego, and body. Like Soula in the Identity Theft parable, expect no warm welcome from your former servant, the mind, when attempting to reclaim your proper place as head of your spiritual household. Your mind, experienced as the ego, will be threatened as you attempt to restore it to its status as servant, after being the undisputed master for so long.

To regain your divine inheritance, know this: *You must first liberate yourself from identifying with your mind or your mind will*

---

* Any personal noun or pronoun in a Wisdom Saying in ALL CAPS is synonymous with SELF, the universal YOU, the Divine, Spirit—the **Eternal YOU**.

In contrast, any personal noun or pronoun in a Wisdom Saying in lowercase refers to one's ordinary personality, personal identity—the **external you**.

46

continue to live its life disguised as the real You! When you begin to doubt yourself, as surely you will from time to time, remember that *nothing can lay permanent claim to or bar you from reclaiming your spiritual inheritance.*

You can and must go home again! You stand at the door of a transformation that will change how you see yourself and expand the vision of your life's possibilities. Enter now and reclaim your *true identity*—that dimension of consciousness where you are whole and happy again.

Following is a treasure trove of additional, original wisdom sayings that represent a measure of the riches I have so far mined during my inward journey. They are designed to bring about a shift in consciousness that will allow you to bypass your conditioned state of mind and reconnect directly with SELF, that mystical, *transformative* power within.

AFFIRMATIVE ACTION

*Say yes to SELF
and live*

AMAZING GRACE

Regardless of your past
you are always on your path

BITTERSWEET

*Sometimes in life
the worst thing that happens
turns out to be your greatest good*

BLACK MAN'S BURDEN

The weight of the past

BLIND AMBITION

*To want to make something of yourself
is to assume that YOU are nothing now*

CAPITAL PUNISHMENT

*Never equate your self worth
with your net worth*

CHILD OF GOD

As Jesus is the SON
surely we are His SISTERS *and* BROTHERS

CHILLING REFLECTION

What you despise in another
is often what you fail to recognize in yourself

COLLATERAL DAMAGE

*You can't maintain a healthy body
with a dis eased mind*

COLLEGE BOUND

Getting a university education
will not open up the Universe to you

COLOR BLIND

*A lot of us see color
and nothing else*

CONSIDER THE SOURCE

*The difference between heaven and hell
is not location
but LIGHT*

CONSPICUOUS CONSUMPTION

More lives are consumed by Fear
than alcohol and drugs combined

CONTAGIOUS DISEASE

*If you are uncomfortable with yourself
you make everyone else uneasy*

CRIME AND PUNISHMENT

When you break the will of another
you both become cripples

CRITICAL MASS

People who say you can't do this or that usually haven't done one or the other

DEAF AND DUMB

*Those who can't hear are deaf
but those who refuse to listen to SPIRIT
are dummies*

DEATH TRAP

A closed mind

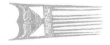

DIAMOND IN THE ROUGH

Each of us faces the same challenge as the diamond cutter
To bring forth inherent strength and beauty
despite the appearance of flaws

DOUBLE STANDARD

How can you be bitter when others reject you
when you refuse to embrace yourself

DRIVING FORCE

*We usually put the past in back of us
instead of behind*

Eating Disorder

One who hates gets consumed

EGO TRIP

*You may have an ego along on your trip
but you don't have to make it your tour guide*

ENEMY WITHIN

Your conditioning

Extreme Makeover

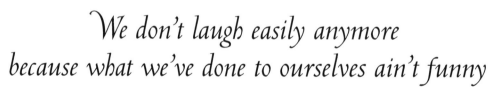

*We don't laugh easily anymore
because what we've done to ourselves ain't funny*

EYE OPENER

Just because your eyes are open
doesn't mean you're wide awake

FATAL ATTRACTION

*Love the person
not your ideal*

FIELD OF DREAMS

*All you can do for people is seed them and weed them
and wait for them to grow*

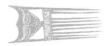

FOR BETTER OR WORSE

Practice makes perfect or imperfect

FOR HEAVEN'S SAKE

Salvation is a function
of how you grow in this life
not who you know in the next

FORM FOLLOWS FUNCTION

If you don't learn to think for yourself
you'll grow up to be a hat rack

FRIENDLY FIRE

*Some of us are here to put out fires
and some of us are here to* LIGHT *them*

FROM HERE TO ETERNITY

*You have an external self
and eternal SELF to embrace*

GAME OF LIFE

You can't be a spectator
in a game that ain't no sport

GREAT DIVIDE

There are those who wish
and those who will

HEART FAILURE

*We often pursue what we believe we lack
rather than what or whom we love*

HEART OF THE MATTER

All that remains of a life well lived
is LOVE

HIGHER AUTHORITY

Most of us aren't ashamed of our actions
but of Others' reactions

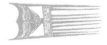

HOLY WAR

*The jihad of lasting peace
transforms who you* **believe** *you are
into who YOU are in truth*

HOME ALONE

If you're living in your head
don't expect many visitors

HOSTILE TAKEOVER

The intellectual
is a hostage of his own mind

HUEMANITY

Your hue ain't YOU

IDENTITY THEFT

*Free your identity
from the prison of your mind
and your authentic life will follow*

ILL GOTTEN GAINS

You ain't makin a livin
if it's sendin you to your grave

IMITATION OF LIFE

We usually commit ourselves to the idea of success but not to successful living

IMMACULATE CONCEPTION

*You must give birth
to the DIVINE in you*

INDECENT EXPOSURE

Nobody looks good enough
to act ugly

INTERNAL CONFLICT

The world is a battlefield
when you're at war with SPIRIT

INVALID

Craving validation
invalidates you

INVISIBLE MAN

The outer directed person
is aware of everything but SELF

IT TAKES ONE TO KNOW ONE

There is a POWER in the universe
that is greater than you
but not other than YOU

JUDGMENT DAY

*We often decide who someone is
without knowing who they are*

KARMA

Life is a boomerang

KIDS ARE US

*Our children are alive
until the adult in us
kills the CHILD in them*

LAST TAG

You can't outrun the problem
when you're it

LEARNING DISORDER

Some women settle for half a man
when they believe they need a man to be whole

LEARNING TREE

Anything learned
can be unlearned

LIBERATION FRONT

*The men we are is often the result
of the women they became*

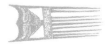

LOOK OF LOVE

We often accept approval
as a substitute for LOVE

LOST AND FOUND

*If death be our end
how did we find each other again*

LOVE

*Anything less
is a mess*

LOVESICK

*Some of us feel we only deserve LOVE
when we are sick*

MAKE NO MISTAKE

*The only mistake
is not to make a mistake*

MASS TRANSIT

Herd minded people are driven

MATTER OF LIFE AND DEATH

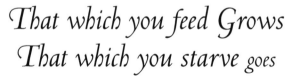

That which you feed Grows
That which you starve goes

MEASURE OF A MAN

Your dreams are as big as you make them
or as small as you believe you are

MENTAL MASTURBATION

*Thinking about living
is a head job*

MIND OVER MATTER

Take the shit the world gives you
and treat it like clay

MIRACLE WORKER

*The way to walk on water
is to wait til it turns to ice*

Mis Education

You can't teach who you don't reach

MISSION IMPOSSIBLE

*Not even the CREATOR
can give you what YOU already have*

NARCOTIC OF HATE

The choice of discriminating people

NATURAL DISASTER

*If you take your gifts for granted
they will turn to stone*

NEAR DEATH EXPERIENCE

*Many of us only decide to live
when the end is in sight*

NEW MESSIAH

Personal Responsibility

No Man's Land

Limbo

ODD COUPLE

*People who are lost
usually find each other*

ONE LOVE

When you love SELF
there is no other

ORIGINAL SIN

Doin the real YOU *in*

OUT OF BODY EXPERIENCE

The only time most of us live our dreams
is when we sleep

OWNER'S MANUAL

If you believe you're a machine
you're bound to breakdown

POWER FAILURE

*The victim will suffer almost any indignity
to maintain the illusion that
someone else is responsible for their life*

POWER OF SUGGESTION

*When you only listen to others
you end up where they've already been*

Profit and Loss

The land of the free
was the home of the Braves

Pros and Cons

You can make life a ball
or a ball and chain

REVERSAL OF FORTUNE

*To claim that life isn't so bad
is to admit you were expecting less*

SAFE SEX

Just because two people aren't doing it doesn't mean they're not making LOVE

SANDS OF TIME

Your body is an hourglass

SECOND BEST

*We get high off life
or the next best thing*

SECOND COMING

*The journey begins with self
and ends with SELF*

SELF INFLICTED WOUND

*You can't deny who YOU are
without leaving a scar*

SEX BIAS

*We are more concerned with kids learning
to manage their behinds
than their minds*

SHIFT HAPPENS

You may not be able to avoid the shit
but you can avoid the stink

SHORT AND SWEET

*Life is short
so make it sweet*

SMALL IS BEAUTIFUL

*Little people are in your life
so you can appreciate the big ones*

SOULMATE

Who YOU are looking for
is looking for YOU

STAR SEARCH

When you stop needing to be seen
you'll discover what it takes to SHINE

STATE OF SUSPENDED ANIMATION

Not failing is not success

STATE OF THE UNION

Many of us sacrifice who we love
on the altar of what we believe

STOP THE KILLING

The time that you're killin
is the time of your life

STRESS FRACTURE

*Don't let the pressure that is meant to make you
break you*

STRIVER'S ROW

*Those who strive to be happy
are not*

SURE THING

The loser knows precisely
what he doesn't want

THOUGHTS ARE SEEDS

Don't plant bitters
and expect to harvest sweets

THOU SHALT KILL

ignorance

TIL DEATH DO US PART

*When the relationship is dead
it's time to part*

TOXIC WASTE

Tryin is like constipation
it ain't shit

TRICK OR TREAT

*If you fail to recognize your blessings
it's cause you're fooled by their disguise*

TRUTH OR CONSEQUENCES

*Live your TRUTH
or die a lie*

VIRGIN TERRITORY

*SELF discovery is a process of exploring
your private parts*

VOICE OF EXPERIENCE

*Kids are our past
we are their future*

VOLUNTARY CONFINEMENT

*By shutting out the world
you imprison the real YOU*

WAGES OF SIN

The one who rejects SPIRIT
has the devil to pay

WAITING TO EXHALE

*If you are preparing to live
you're not yet alive*

WAKE UP CALL

You can choose not to answer the call of destiny
but you'll still have to pay for that Call

WAR ROOM

Your mind

WEAPON OF MASS DESTRUCTION

False beliefs

WEATHER ADVISORY

As long as your outlook is overcast
you'll be under the weather

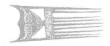

WEIGHT OF THE WORLD

*Self worth can never be accurately weighed
on another's scale*

WHAT YOU SEE IS WHAT YOU GET

*You can't exceed
your vision of yourself*

WHITE MAN'S BURDEN

The sin of skin

WISDOM

Heartsmart

WITHOUT A DOUBT

If you're living in doubt
watch out

WORLDLY WISE

Those who are happily occupied in this life
are seldom preoccupied with the next

YEAST OF LIFE

*A soul without humor
is like unleavened bread*

YOU ARE IT

*YOU are GOD
disguised as you*

YOUR BETTER HALF

The half that makes you WHOLE

Know Thy Self

The great spiritual task is not to change people but to help them change how they see themselves

To many, the statement "I am God" sings of blasphemy. God, according to conventional religion, is the supreme deity, the almighty eternal omniscient creator. How can any lowly human being claim that he or she is God? . . .

Yet when mystics say, "I am God" or words to that effect, they are not talking of an individual person. Their inner explorations have revealed the true nature of the Self, and it is this that they identify with God. They are claiming that the essence of self, the sense of "I am" without any personal attributes, is God.

Peter Russell
Author, *From Science to God*

We all listen to the god within us.

Miriam-Rose Ungunmerr
Indigenous Australian Elder

Make yourself the object of intense study and you will discover God.

ANCIENT EGYPTIAN PROVERB

This is your Self, that is within all; everything else but This is perishable.

BIRHADARANYAKA UPANISHAD

Sacred Hindu Scripture

When we are in touch with the highest spirit in ourselves, we too are a Buddha, filled with the Holy Spirit.

Thich Nhat Hanh

Buddhist Monk

Everyone is sacred. You're sacred and I'm sacred. Every time you blink your eye, or I blink my eye, God blinks His eye. God sees through your eyes and my eyes. We are sacred.

Mathew King, Chief Noble Red Man

Lakota Sioux

All humans possess what is known as 'Ayammo' (destiny or fate) and are expected to eventually become one with Spirit, with Oludumare (Orun, the divine creator and source of all energy).

YORUBA RELIGION

Beside the river stands the holy tree of life; there doth my father dwell, and my home is in him.
The heavenly father and I are one.

THE ESSENE GOSPEL OF PEACE
Early Jewish Sect

I have said, Ye are gods; and all of you are children of the most High.

Asaph
Psalm 82:6, KJV

Neither shall they say, Lo here! or, lo there! for, behold, the kingdom of God is within you.

Jesus of Nazareth
Luke 17:21, KJV

When the soul loves something it becomes like unto it . . . if it should love God does it not become God?

Saint Augustine
Early Christian Theologian

You are not this body, you are not this mind, you are Spirit . . . this is the greatest truth.
Shri Mataji Nirmala Devi
Hindu Yogi

The life within you is God; whatever is true of God is true of your life, since your life and the life of God are not two but one.

Ernest Holmes
Founder, Religious Science

I AM is the name of God . . . God is none other than the Self.
Sri Ramana Maharshi
Hindu Sage

. . . an awareness within each soul, imprinted in pattern on the mind and waiting to be awakened by the will, of the soul's oneness with God.

Edgar Cayce
Founder, Association for Research and Enlightenment

The ultimate mystical experience is of one's identity with the divine power. That divinity is actually your innermost being.

Joseph Campbell
Mythologist

The recognition of God is the recognition of yourself.

Helen Schucman
Author, *A Course in Miracles*

The twenty-first century will be the time of awakenings, of meeting The Creator Within. Many beings will experience Oneness with God and all of life.

Neale Donald Walsch
Author, *Conversations with God*

Even belief in God is a poor substitute for the living reality of God manifesting every moment of your life.

Eckhart Tolle
Spiritual Teacher

Stop looking outside for help. You're sourced and fueled by a renewable resource, which is within you. It never runs out. It is your Essence.

Rev. Michael Beckwith
Founder, Agape International Spiritual Center

Who am I? The thought free observer (infinite consciousness); an infinite being pretending to be a person.

Deepak Chopra, MD
Founder, Alliance for a New Humanity

My confidence comes from knowing there is a power greater than myself that I am a part of and it is a part of me.

Oprah Winfrey
Spiritual Media Pioneer

Man is asleep—must he die before he wakes up?

Indries Shah
Sufi (Islamic) Scholar

Still having trouble seeing yourself as God? Try this: Imagine God as the ocean. If you take a bucket of water out of the ocean, is the water in the bucket the ocean? Yes, indeed, it is all together ocean—and the ocean though it is larger is still altogether the whole of the ocean in the bucket. Now think of yourself as a bucket of God. Altogether God; and God altogether you. It is only when you stay separated from the ocean that the water dries up.

Dr. Wayne Dyer
Author, *Wishes Fulfilled*

Our deepest fear is not that we are inadequate. Our deepest fear is that we are powerful beyond measure. It is our light, not our darkness, that most frightens us.

Marianne Williamson
Author, *A Return to Love*

Key Terms

Divine estate—The dimension of consciousness where one is whole, lacking nothing to be complete, and at peace; synonymous with *Self*—the **KINGDOM WITHIN**

Headly—(with uppercase "H") The conditioned mind or state when operating from a position of dominance in pursuit of an agenda apart from the interest of the individual—the **MATRIX MASTER**

headly—(with lowercase "h") The conditioned mind or state that functions in the interest of the individual—the **PERSONAL COMPUTER**

hego—The aspect of mind that steals its host's identity by substituting itself for one's true identity; synonymous with ego, false self, mind-made self, false identity—the **GREAT PRETENDER**

Self—(with uppercase "S") The *limitless, spiritual Consciousness*; the transpersonal center that reflects one's *true identity*; synonymous with Source, Spirit, Presence, Healer, the Divine, God, Creator, Supreme Guide, the real or universal You—the **TRANSFORMER**

self—(with lowercase "s") The limited, ego-driven consciousness; one's personality that is *transformed* through contact with the spiritual energy of the Self—the **CATERPILLAR**

Soula—(with uppercase "S") The person who, unaware they are already whole, succumbs to the belief they are missing something to make their life complete that can only be found in the world outside—the **BLIND BELIEVER**

soula—(with lowercase "s") The diminished condition of the person who, so driven by their obsession to find that "missing something," forgets their true identity (asleep to Self) and becomes a victim of identity theft—the **SLEEP WALKER**

Acknowledgments

Recognizing the following individuals does not suggest that they are in agreement with everything I have expressed in this book. My heartfelt thanks to Ranjit Bhattacharya for being a worthy traveling companion, scribe, and my ears when I failed to hear; Victoria Caldwell, who helped spark the idea for **Life Is Funny but It Ain't No Joke** during our garden talk; Crystal D. Cubbage, my literary midwife whose amazing work ethic and unfailing encouragement made the delivery of the first drafts possible; my long-suffering wife, Gerri, who through her sage advice, constant encouragement, and *patience*, as well as her typing skill, ensured that my manuscript finally reached the publisher; and Mark Parker Miller, book production manager, who without complaint patiently and skillfully guided me through every grueling step of the publishing process.

My sincere gratitude also to those who gave generously of their expertise, wise advice, or encouragement: Samer Abdalla, Irv Ackelsberg, Vernice Bond, Martin V. Burrows, Jeff Carreira, Dr. Robert Chapman, Larry Cohen, Tidiane Diop, Calista Dorsey, Shelby Durham-Jackson, Dawn Fant-Fleurizard, Jerome Gladden, David Haines, Ethel Hendricks, Rae Scott Jones, Kevin A. King, Leslie S. King, Darien Marshall, Jeremy May, Atiba McLean, Edgar A. Mitchell Jr., Greg Naylor, Thomas F. Powell Jr., MD, Samuel Pressley, Samuel Reynolds, Sergio Rozzelle, Cornelius Simpkins, Carolyn Simpson, Sandy Smith, Numa St. Louis, Warren Tanksley, David Thompson, Steve Ushioda, Darlene Walker, Rana Walker, Tschaka Walker, Richard Watson, Eric C. Webb, Reggie White, and JoAnne Woods.

Finally, I owe a profound debt of thanks to those whose names are not listed but whose contributions are no less appreciated. You know who you are.

Word about the Author

REGINALD E. WALKER is a teacher, life coach, and spiritual guide. He developed *Mind Power,* the first course of its kind offered at his alma mater, the University of Pennsylvania. He conducts Self rediscovery and self development workshops and seminars for domestic and international organizations. The guiding principle of RegE's life work is, *The great spiritual task is not to change people but to help them change how they see themselves.* He lived with his family in Ghana, West Africa, and presently resides in his hometown, Philadelphia, Pennsylvania, with his wife, Gerri. Visit him at www.harmanitypress.com.

Photo: John Creveling

RegE welcomes the opportunity to speak to your group. Contact him or inquire about bulk order discounts via www.harmanitypress.com. This book is available from Amazon.com and other retail outlets and as a Kindle ebook.

Made in the USA
Middletown, DE
13 June 2020

97836242R00120